The Whooping Crane

Written and Illustrated
by
J. M. Roever

Steck-Vaughn Company
An Intext Publisher

Austin, Texas

ISBN 0-8114-7721-5
Library of Congress Catalog Card Number 79-139290
Copyright © 1971 by Steck-Vaughn Company, Austin, Texas
All Rights Reserved
Printed and Bound in the United States of America

The Whooping Crane

A strange noise echoes across the salt marshes like the harsh bugling notes of a toy horn or the war whoop of an ancient Indian warrior. This spine-tingling call is the voice of one of the rarest birds in our country—the majestic whooping crane.

Common Crane—about 4 feet tall (Europe and Asia)

Types of Cranes

There are 14 known species of cranes in the world. Two species of cranes are found in North America, the whooping cranes and the sandhill cranes. In South America there are no cranes at all.

Whooping Crane—almost 5 feet tall (North America)

Demoiselle Crane—about 3 feet tall (Asia, Europe, and Africa)

Crowned Crane—about 3 feet tall (Africa)

Sarus Crane—almost 5 feet tall (India and China to the Philippines)

Sandhill Crane—about 4 feet tall (North America)

The whooping crane is the tallest bird in North America. It struts on stiltlike legs in a haughty manner —step left, pause; step right, pause; step left, pause. The whooping crane's fully spread wings sometimes measure 7½ feet from tip to tip.

Air from lungs of whooping crane enters here.

Coiled Windpipe

French Horn

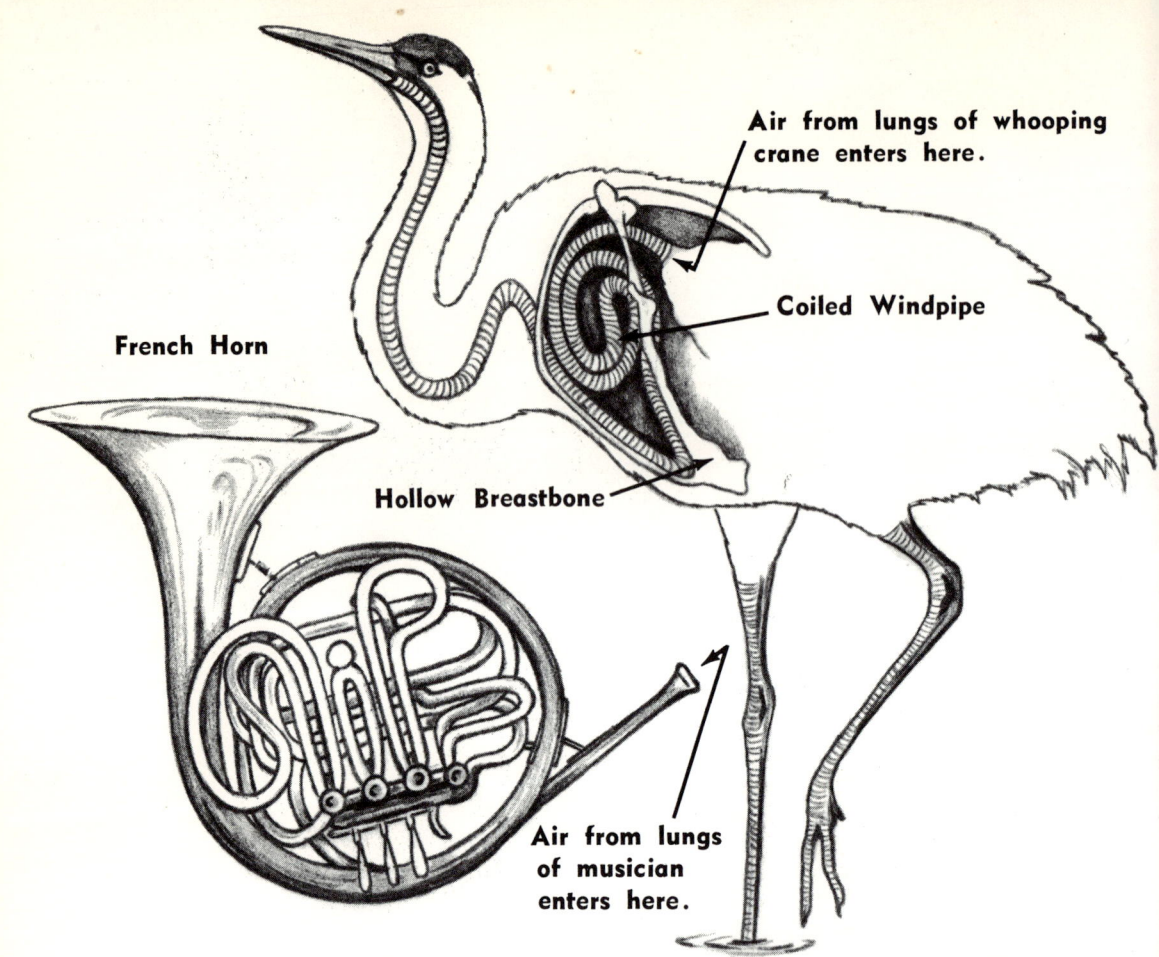

Hollow Breastbone

Air from lungs of musician enters here.

If disturbed or angered, the whooping crane makes its loud whooping call. The unusual noise can be heard more than a mile away. The whooping crane's call comes from a hollow neck passage called a windpipe. The crane's windpipe is longer than its entire neck. Part of the windpipe is coiled like a French horn deep in a hollow portion of the whooping crane's breast.

Life History of the Whooping Crane

Deep in the wilderness of Canada's Northwest Territories, the life of a whooping crane begins. In late May or June the adult cranes build a nest in a clump of protected marsh grass. Normally 2 eggs are laid in the nest. For about 34 days the parents take turns sitting on the eggs to keep them warm.

The newly hatched whooping crane chicks are covered with soft reddish down.

Whooping Crane Chick—about 2½ weeks old

Whooping Crane Chick—about 5 weeks old

Whooping Crane Chick—about 4 days old; smaller than an adult robin

**Whooping Crane
3 months old**

**Whooping Crane
4½ months old**

    As the young cranes grow, new feathers replace the soft baby down. These feathers have a mixed color of grayish white and brownish red. Sometimes the young cranes look almost pink. Scientists call these feathers the juvenile plumage.

    When immature whooping cranes are about 4 months old, the Canadian summer ends. Cold weather approaches, and the young birds fly south with their parents.

Migration

Birds that fly from one section of the country to another, according to the seasons, are called migratory birds. Ducks, geese, robins, swallows, and cranes are some well-known migratory birds.

Whooping cranes migrate from the wilderness of northern Canada to the coastal marshes of Texas.

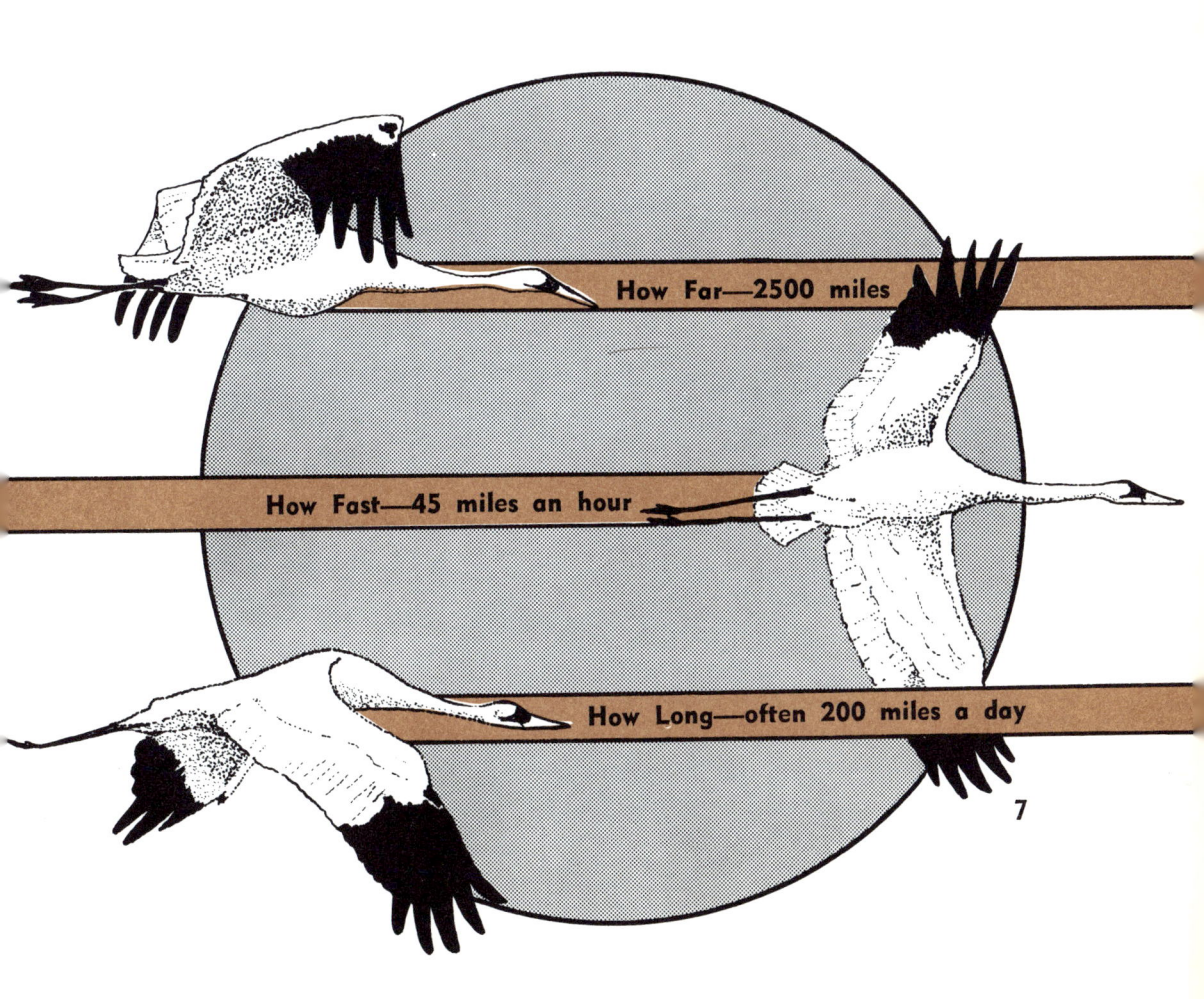

How Far—2500 miles

How Fast—45 miles an hour

How Long—often 200 miles a day

Whooping cranes migrate in family groups. They fly with their long necks extended and their long black legs stretched out behind them. Sometimes when the air currents are right, the whooping cranes join in a breathtaking performance. Circling and diving, they swoop back and forth in the sky, and their majestic white wings flash and sparkle in a beautiful aerial ballet.

9

One by one the whooping crane families arrive at their winter feeding grounds in the Texas coastal marshes. Each family group quickly selects a home territory. The area occupied by one whooping crane family often covers 400 acres of marshland and water. Different crane families often fight over invisible boundary lines that divide each territory.

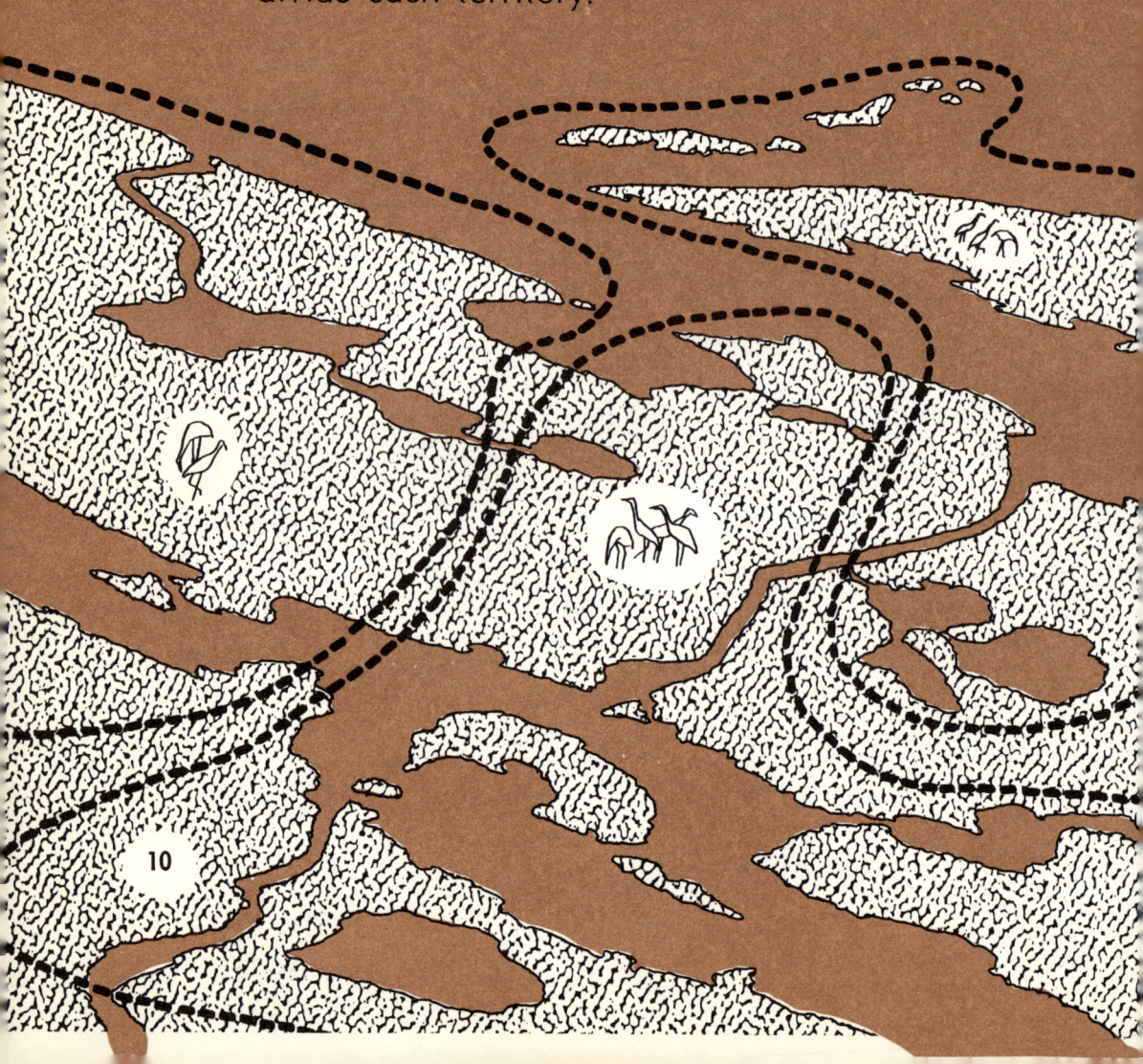

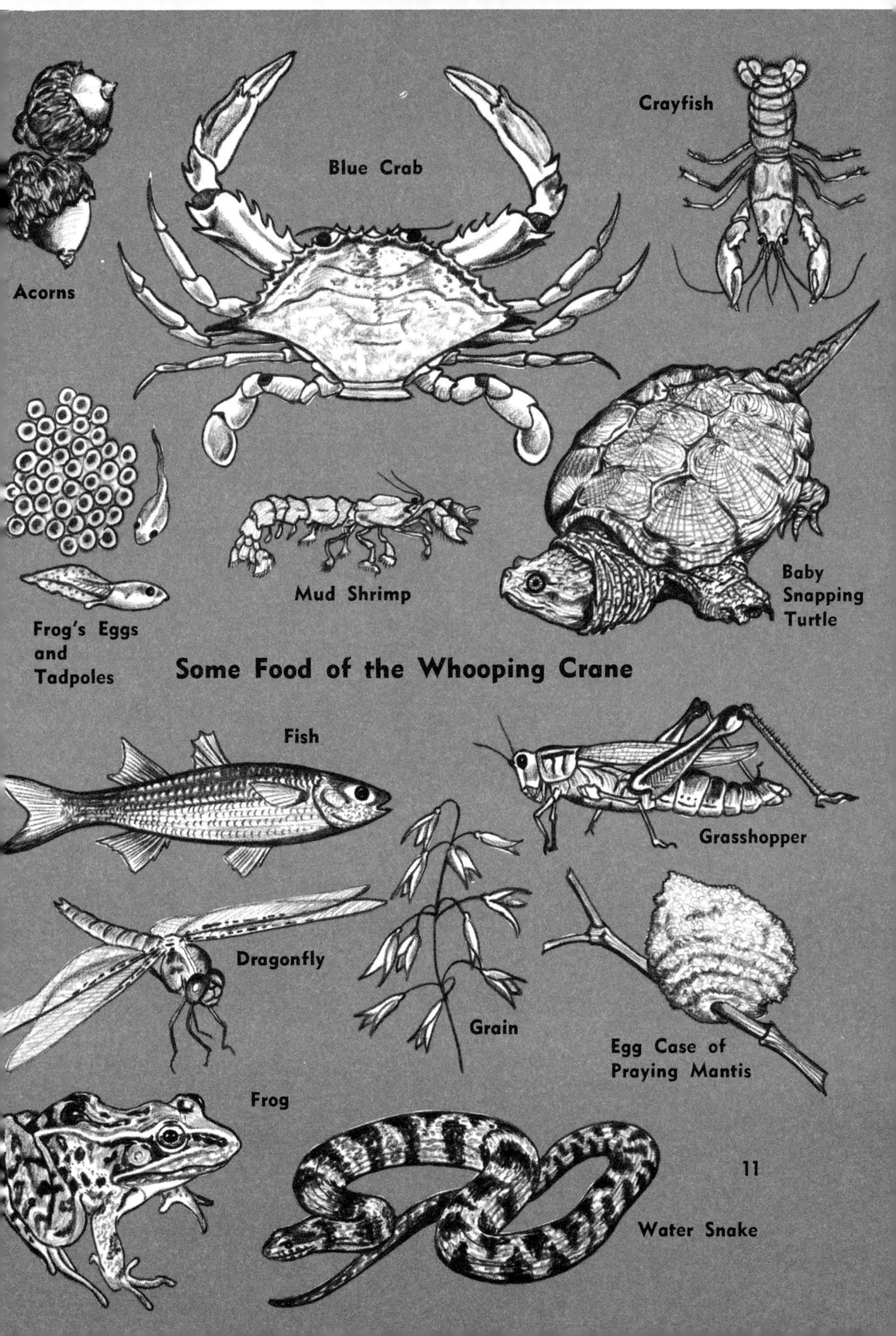

Some Food of the Whooping Crane

Acorns
Blue Crab
Crayfish
Frog's Eggs and Tadpoles
Mud Shrimp
Baby Snapping Turtle
Fish
Grasshopper
Dragonfly
Grain
Egg Case of Praying Mantis
Frog
Water Snake

Spring in the Texas Coastal Marshes

When the warm winds of spring blow over the Texas marshlands, the whooping cranes become restless. They sense that winter is ending in their Canadian nesting grounds. The young cranes lose their juvenile plumage. Their new feathers are white like the plumage of the adult birds. Suddenly, the parent whooping cranes chase their full-grown offspring away.

As the time for spring migration nears, the adult birds perform the courtship dance of the whooping cranes. Nodding his head and flapping his wings, the male crane struts toward his mate. He skips back and forth before the female crane and then leaps high into the air. His legs are stiff, his neck is arched over his back, and his bill is pointed toward the sky. The female crane suddenly joins him, and the birds do the dance together.

13

Early History of Whooping Cranes

Thousands of years ago, when the last glaciers had disappeared from North America, large areas of water covered the land. Great flocks of whooping cranes stalked through the marshes. As the years passed, the marshes began to dry up, and forests grew in their place. The flocks of whooping cranes slowly grew smaller. Most of the great birds settled in the coastal marshes of Texas and Louisiana. The Louisiana whooping cranes were unusual, because they did not migrate.

The rest of the cranes migrated every spring to the wide prairie marshes. There they built their nests and raised their young. Undisturbed and undiscovered, the whooping cranes survived in the marshes until the exploration of the New World.

When the pioneers, trappers, farmers, and hunters settled the wilderness of North America, the whooping cranes rapidly disappeared. The great prairie marshes were drained to make wheat fields and grazing lands. The marshy grasslands of Louisiana were changed into rice fields.

Looking for a safe place to raise their chicks, the remaining cranes flew off into the wilderness of northern Canada. For more than 30 years no one knew where the great birds were hiding their nests. But every winter the whooping cranes flew south to the marshes of the Gulf coast. Sometimes they brought a few young cranes with them. But often they returned fewer in number than before.

Passenger Pigeon
(extinct since 1914)

Heath Hen
(extinct since 1933)

Extinct and Endangered North American Birds

In 1940 a violent hurricane blew the Louisiana whooping cranes out of their marsh. A few years later the wild Louisiana cranes were gone forever. When biologists counted all the whooping cranes in 1941, only 15 wild whoopers were left. The whooping crane almost became extinct.

Many North American birds are so rare that they may become extinct. They are described as endangered wildlife.

Whooping Crane
(endangered)

Bald Eagle
(endangered)

Labrador Duck
(extinct since 1878)

Great Auk
(extinct since 1844)

Ivory-Billed Woodpecker
(endangered)

California Condor
(endangered)

Extinct (ek-stinkt)—having no survivors

Steps To Save the Whoopers

In 1916 the governments of the United States and Great Britain signed the Migratory Bird Treaty. The treaty made it illegal to kill whooping cranes in the United States and Canada. Then in 1937 the United States government purchased a portion of the Texas marshland as a safe winter home for the whooping cranes. Today this sanctuary is called the Aransas National Wildlife Refuge.

In the United States, National Wildlife Refuges are marked with this sign of the flying Canada Goose.

NATIONAL WILDLIFE REFUGE

U. S. DEPARTMENT OF THE INTERIOR
FISH AND WILDLIFE SERVICE
BUREAU OF
SPORT FISHERIES AND WILDLIFE

UNAUTHORIZED ENTRY PROHIBITED

Difficult Years for Cranes

Even in the twentieth century the whooping cranes were not entirely safe from man's activities. At Aransas a deep channel for boats, part of the Gulf Intracoastal Waterway, was dredged through the once quiet salt marshes. Soon hunters, fishermen, and sightseers traveled by water into the whooping cranes' feeding grounds. Oil wells were drilled in the sand flats. The noise from private planes and a nearby bombing and machine-gun target range shattered the stillness of the wildlife sanctuary.

Rain

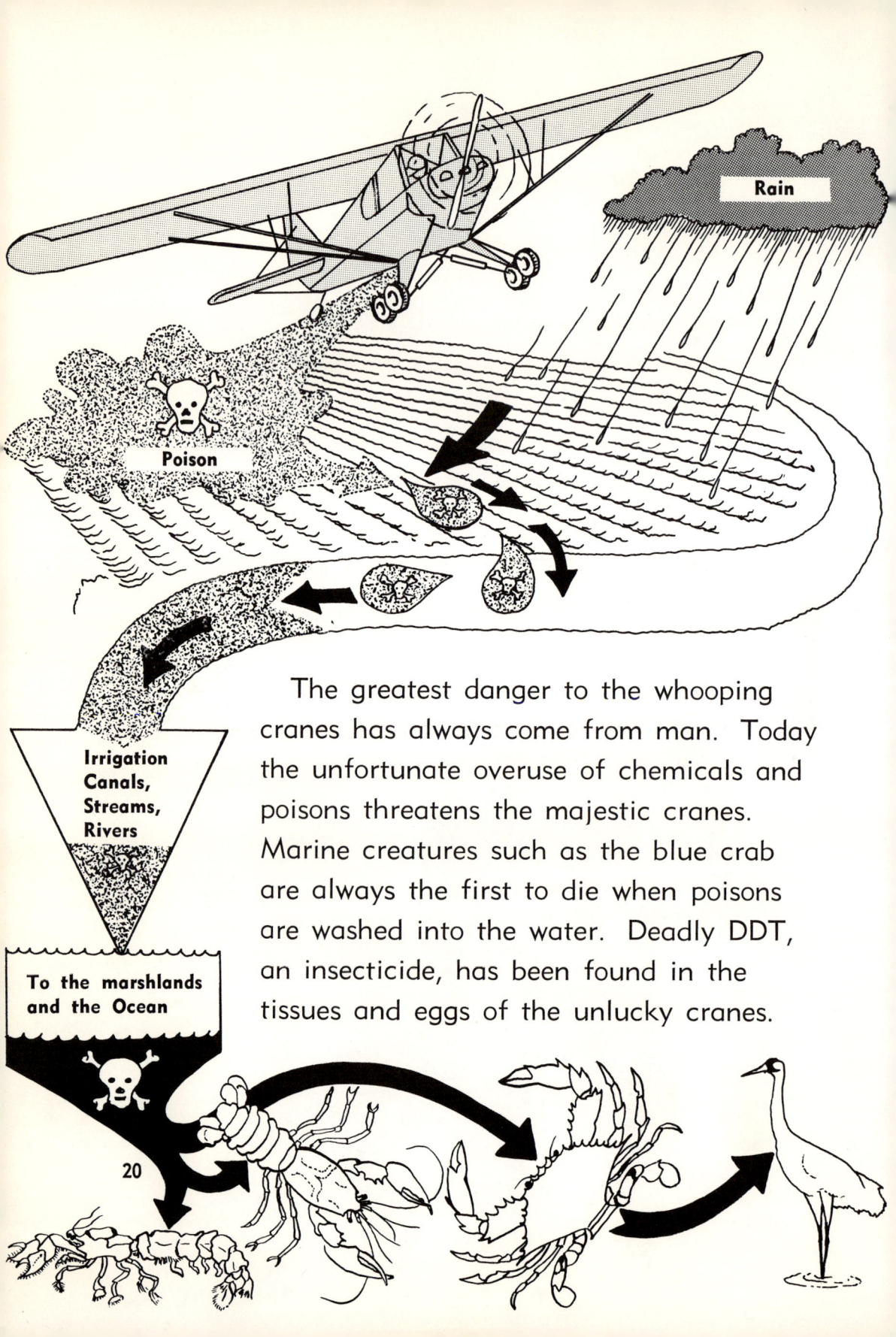

Poison

Irrigation Canals, Streams, Rivers

To the marshlands and the Ocean

The greatest danger to the whooping cranes has always come from man. Today the unfortunate overuse of chemicals and poisons threatens the majestic cranes. Marine creatures such as the blue crab are always the first to die when poisons are washed into the water. Deadly DDT, an insecticide, has been found in the tissues and eggs of the unlucky cranes.

Robert Porter Allen, 1905-1963

No book about whooping cranes would be complete without telling about Robert Porter Allen, the whooping cranes' hard-working friend. For two years Mr. Allen gathered information for a report about the endangered cranes. During the winter he watched and studied the whooping cranes at Aransas. In the summer he searched for their hidden nests in the Canadian wilderness.

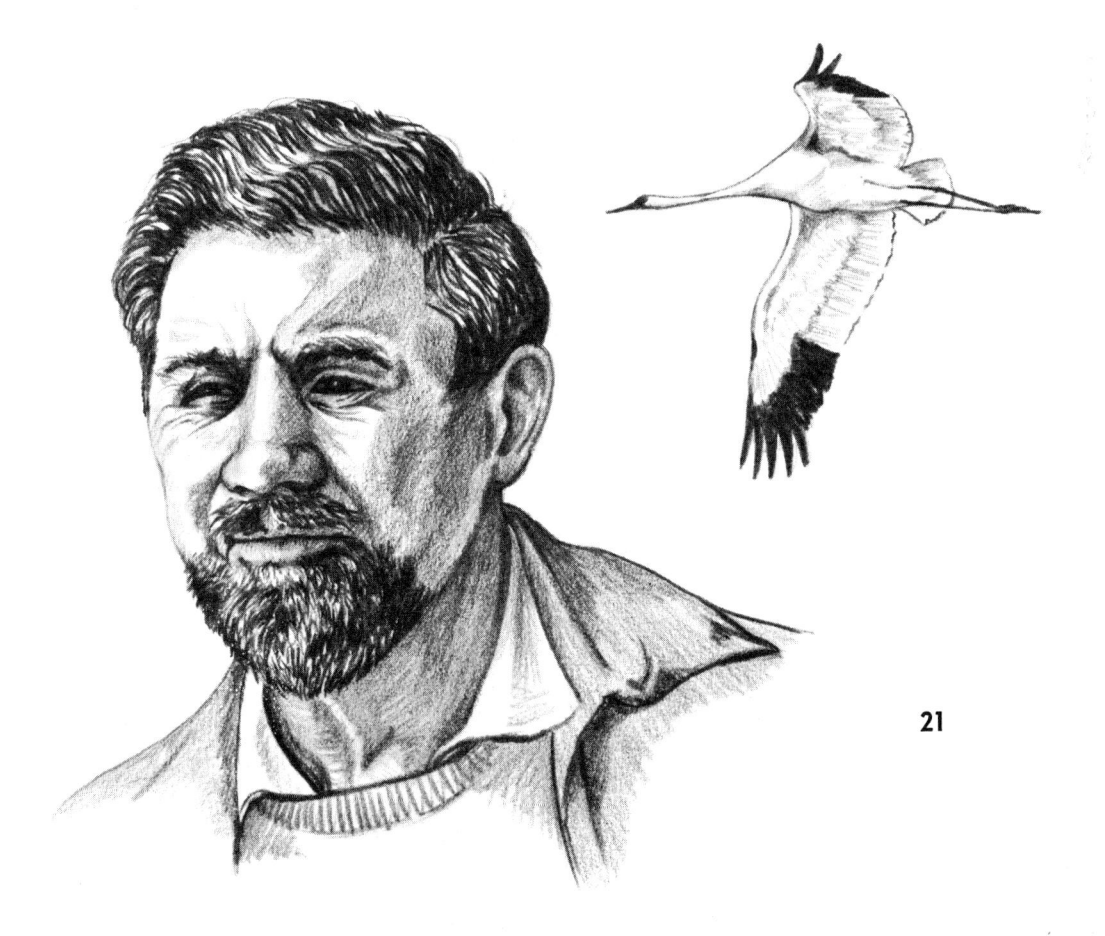

A Forest Fire Discovery

In the summer of 1954, a fire broke out in Wood Buffalo National Park, which is near Great Slave Lake in the Canadian Northwest Territories. A pilot from the Canadian Forest Service spotted a group of whooping cranes as he returned from the fire. The following spring Mr. Allen and two other men traveled into the wilderness of Wood Buffalo National Park. On a muddy bank the men found the treasure that they had been searching for—the 7-inch footprints of an adult whooping crane with the tiny prints of a young crane nearby.

Cranes in Captivity

Because not many people had an opportunity to see the wild cranes, they gave all their attention to the only cranes they could visit—the cranes in captivity. The most famous of all captive whooping cranes was Josephine, "the Dowager Queen of the Cranes." Josephine had been found by a farmer after the hurricane in 1940.

She was the lone survivor of the nonmigratory Louisiana flock. For 24 years Josephine lived at the Audubon Park Zoo in New Orleans.

Josephine and Crip, a captive male whooping crane, successfully raised four chicks. Josephine's offspring live in the Audubon Park Zoo.

In April 1956 a female whooping crane flew into a high wire in Texas and damaged her wing. She was rescued by a rancher and sent to the San Antonio Zoo. There she was nicknamed Rosie. After Josephine's death, Rosie became Crip's new mate, and in 1967 Rosie and Crip raised a male whooping crane named Tex.

A Bold New Plan

After the births of the baby cranes at the zoos, many people recommended that whooping cranes be raised in captivity. They hoped that the offspring of captive cranes could be set free again.

A bold new plan was drawn up by the Canadian Wildlife Service and the United States Department of the Interior. In 1967 biologists flew to Wood Buffalo National Park. They took 6 eggs from different whooping crane nests.

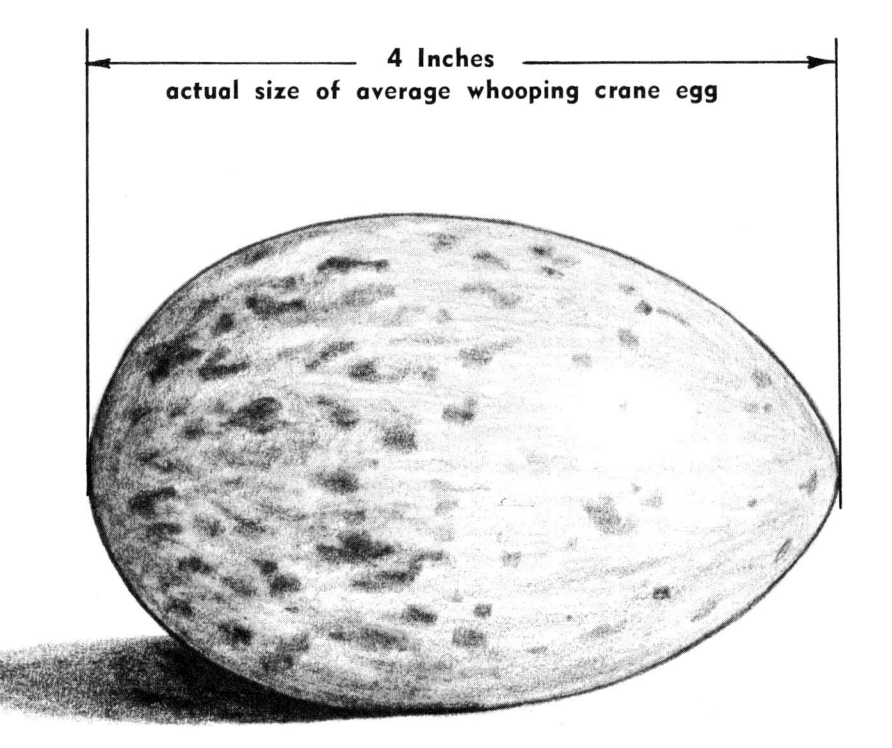

4 Inches
actual size of average whooping crane egg

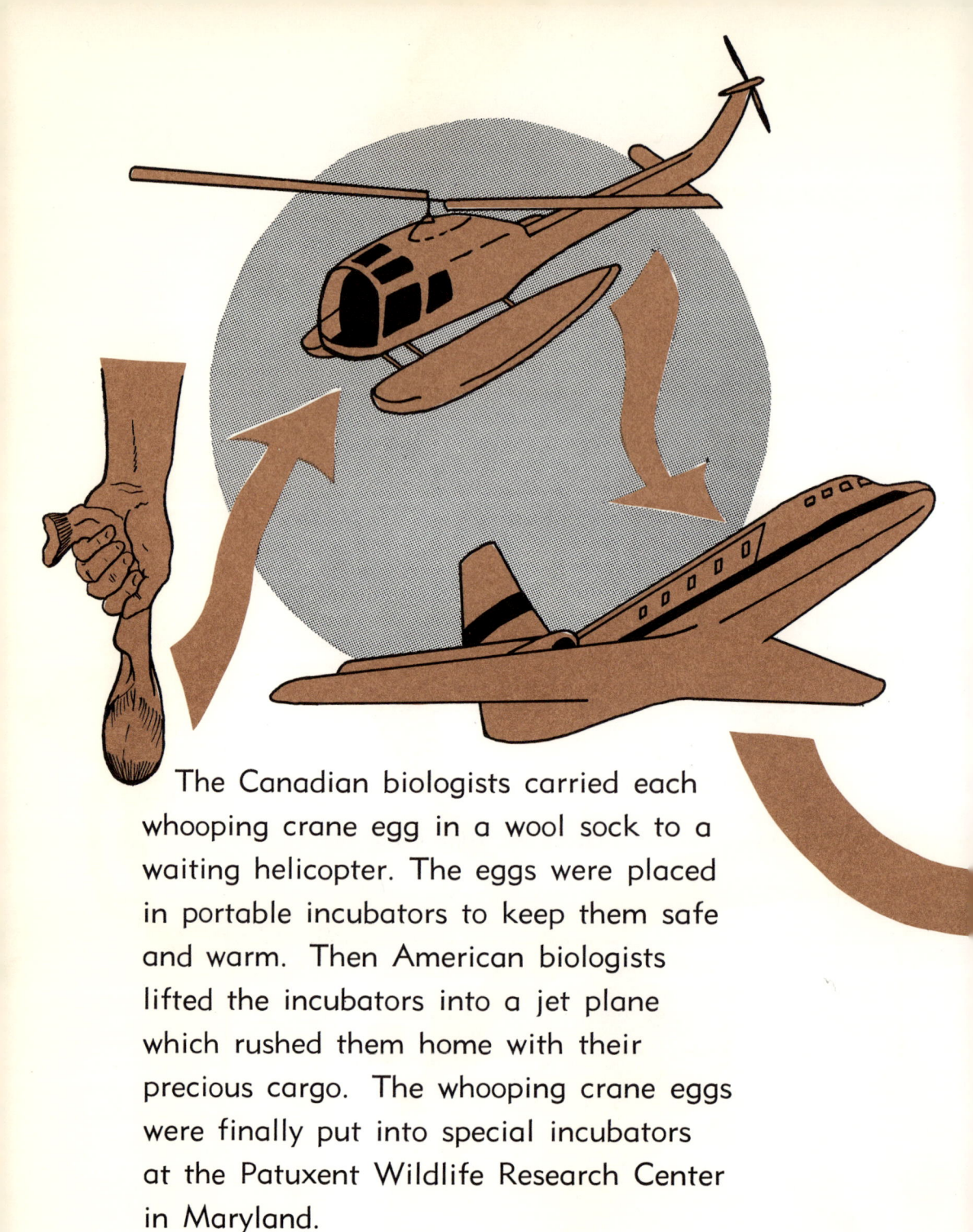

The Canadian biologists carried each whooping crane egg in a wool sock to a waiting helicopter. The eggs were placed in portable incubators to keep them safe and warm. Then American biologists lifted the incubators into a jet plane which rushed them home with their precious cargo. The whooping crane eggs were finally put into special incubators at the Patuxent Wildlife Research Center in Maryland.

Patuxent Wildlife Research Center

When the whooping crane eggs hatched at Patuxent, the downy chicks received as much attention as human babies. Their food was specially prepared and their pens carefully warmed.

Two other male whooping cranes were brought to live at Patuxent. One was Rosie's offspring, Tex, and the other was Canus, who was found injured on the Canadian nesting grounds. His name is formed from the names of his two countries.

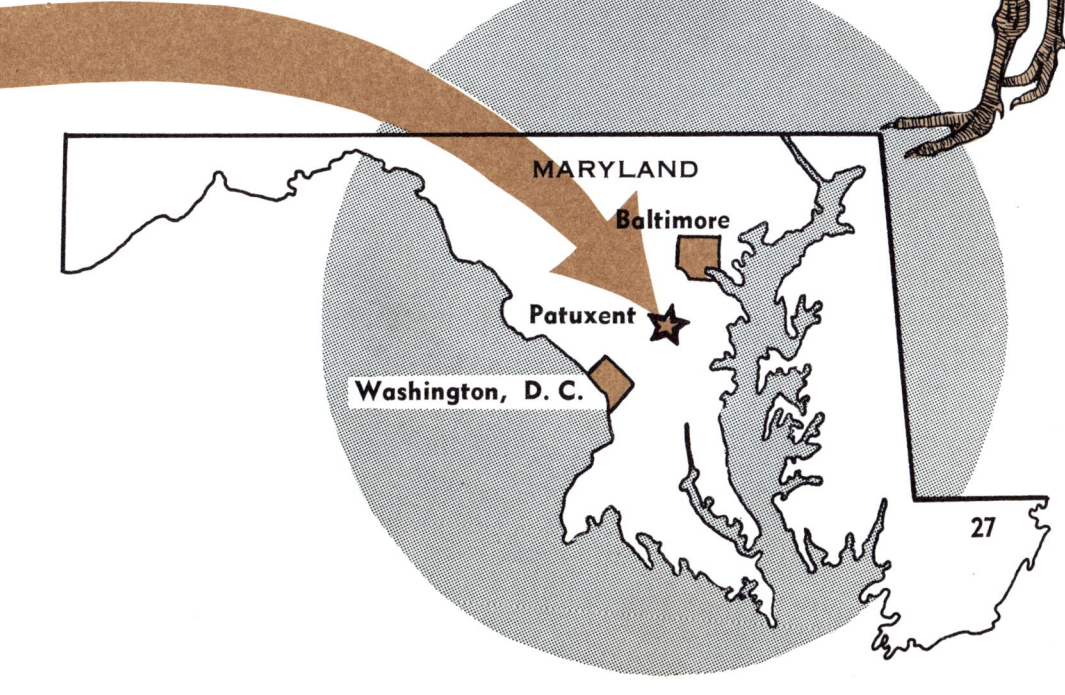

A Life History Map of the Whooping Cranes

                                                              PAGE

1. Wood Buffalo National Park—
   the nesting ground 22, 25
2. Great Slave Lake 22
3. Aransas National Wildlife Refuge—
   winter home 18, 19, 21
4. San Antonio Zoo—home of Rosie and Crip 24
5. Audubon Park Zoo, New Orleans 23, 24
6. Patuxent Wildlife Research Center 26, 27
7. Former prairie nesting grounds of the cranes ... 15
8. Migration route of the whooping cranes 7
9. White Lake, Louisiana—home of the
   now extinct flock of nonmigratory
   whooping cranes 14, 17, 23
10. Gulf of Mexico
11. Matagorda Island—site of bombing range 19
12. San Antonio Bay
13. Gulf Intracoastal Waterway 19
14. St. Charles Bay
15. Highway 35 to Corpus Christi, Texas
16. Town of Austwell, Texas
17. Aransas Bay

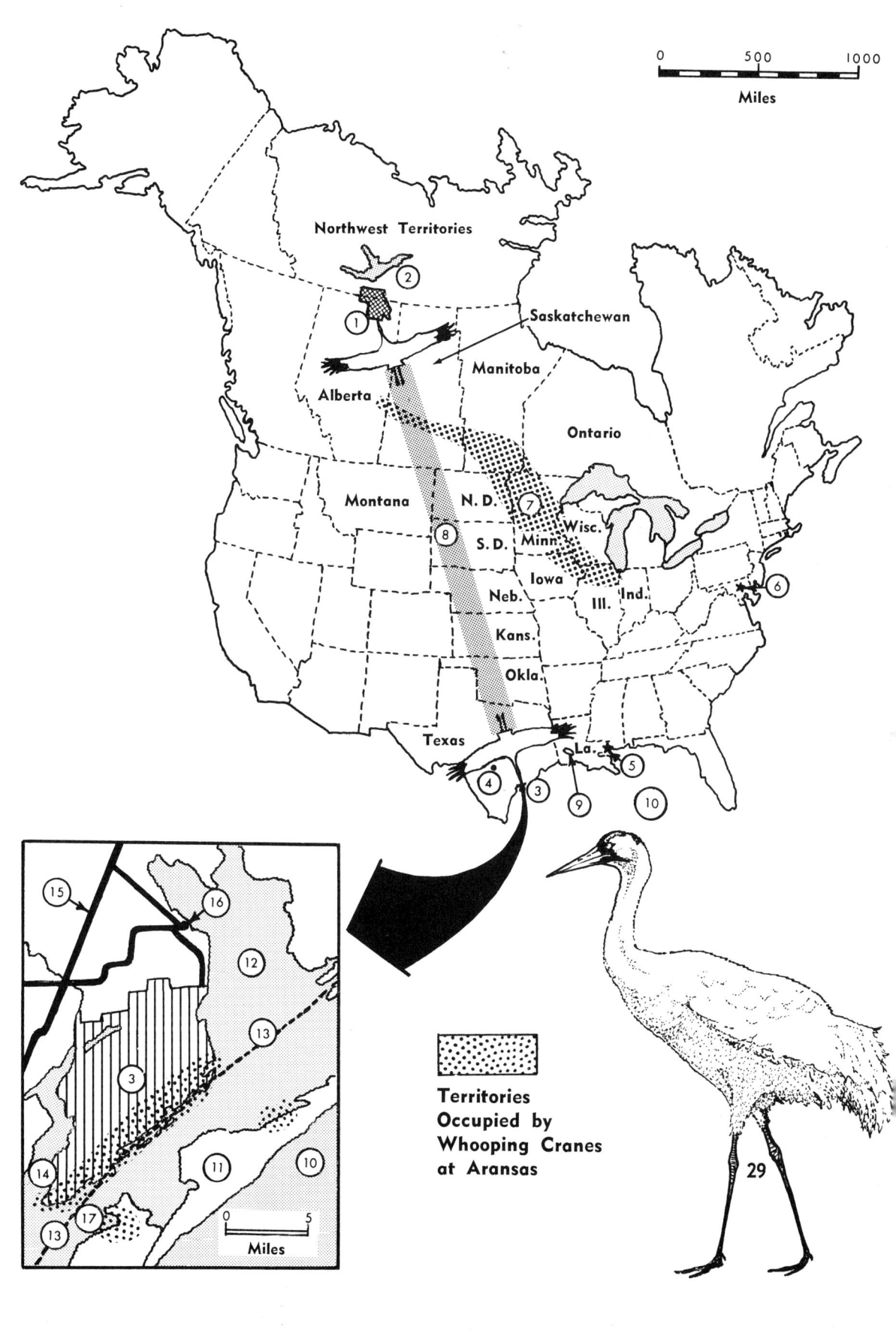

Territories Occupied by Whooping Cranes at Aransas

New Hope for the Wild Whooping Cranes

The Canadian "eggnapping" experiment has not prevented the wild adult whooping cranes from successfully hatching the remaining eggs in their nests. In 1967 the adult cranes brought 9 new young cranes with them to Aransas.

Today there is new hope for the future of the wild whooping cranes. They have come from the brink of extinction, a mere 15 birds in 1941 to a reassuring total of 57 in 1970. The strange call of the whooping crane still drifts across the marshes as it did when Robert Porter Allen wrote, "As they move . . . there is a dignity and a sense of unconquered wildness . . . an obstinate will to survive."